ENGAGING MINDS
IN English Language Arts Classrooms

Engaging Minds in the Classroom: The Surprising Power of Joy
by Michael F. Opitz and Michael P. Ford

Engaging Minds in Science and Math Classrooms: The Surprising Power of Joy
by Eric Brunsell and Michelle A. Fleming
edited by Michael F. Opitz and Michael P. Ford

Engaging Minds in Social Studies Classrooms: The Surprising Power of Joy
by James A. Erekson
edited by Michael F. Opitz and Michael P. Ford

ENGAGING MINDS

IN English Language Arts Classrooms

THE SURPRISING POWER OF **JOY**

MARY JO FRESCH

Edited by
Michael F. Opitz & Michael P. Ford

ASCD

Alexandria, Virginia USA

1703 N. Beauregard St. • Alexandria, VA 22311-1714 USA
Phone: 800-933-2723 or 703-578-9600 • Fax: 703-575-5400
Website: www.ascd.org • E-mail: member@ascd.org
Author guidelines: www.ascd.org/write

Gene R. Carter, *Executive Director*; Richard Papale, *Acting Chief Program Development Officer*; Stefani Roth, *Interim Publisher*; Laura Lawson and Stefani Roth, *Acquisitions Editors*; Julie Houtz, *Director, Book Editing & Production*; Darcie Russell, *Senior Associate Editor*; Georgia Park, *Senior Graphic Designer*; Mike Kalyan, *Production Manager*; Barton Matheson Willse & Worthington, *Typesetter*; Andrea Wilson, *Production Specialist*

Printed in the United States of America. Cover art © 2014 ASCD. ASCD publications present a variety of viewpoints. The views expressed or implied in this book should not be interpreted as official positions of the Association. All referenced trademarks are the property of their respective owners.

All web links in this book are correct as of the publication date below but may have become inactive or otherwise modified since that time. If you notice a deactivated or changed link, please e-mail books@ascd.org with the words "Link Update" in the subject line. In your message, please specify the web link, the book title, and the page number on which the link appears.

PAPERBACK ISBN: 978-1-4166-1725-9 ASCD product #113021   n1/14

Also available as an e-book (see Books in Print for the ISBNs).

Quantity discounts: 10–49 copies, 10%; 50+ copies, 15%; for 1,000 or more copies, call 800-933-2723, ext. 5634, or 703-575-5634. For desk copies: www.ascd.org/deskcopy

Library of Congress Cataloging-in-Publication Data

Fresch, Mary Jo, 1952–
    Engaging minds in English language arts classrooms : the surprising power of joy / Mary Jo Fresch ; Michael F. Opitz and Michael P. Ford, eds.
       pages   cm
    Includes bibliographical references and index.
    ISBN 978-1-4166-1725-9
 1. Language arts—Psychological aspects.   2. Motivation in education.   3. Effective teaching.
 I. Opitz, Michael F., editor of compilation.   II. Ford, Michael P., editor of compilation.   III. Title.
    LB1576.F733 2014
    372.6—dc23
                                                                              2013041447

23 22 21 20 19 18 17 16 15 14   1 2 3 4 5 6 7 8 9 10 11 12

ENGAGING MINDS
in English Language Arts Classrooms

THE SURPRISING POWER OF **JOY**

Acknowledgments

I'd like to thank Mike Opitz and Mike Ford for their vision of these joyful learning and teaching books. It was a joy to craft this book. Special, loving thanks to my grandchildren, who inspire me to make joyful learning important to every teacher.

Introduction

What is it that really engages students in learning? How can we keep students attentive, thoughtful, and inquisitive about learning? In their foundational book for this series, *Engaging Minds in the Classroom: The Surprising Power of Joy* (2014), Michael F. Opitz and Michael P. Ford noted that "if we truly want to advance the learning of all students, we need to seriously consider how noncognitive skills influence learning" (p. 3). *Noncognitive skills* include attributes such as resilience, perseverance, self-control, and curiosity; encouraging students to develop these affective dimensions of learning is, basically, what joyful learning (and joyful teaching) is all about. After years of language arts presentations about spelling, word study, and the history of the English language, I've identified five key principles that collectively contribute to the joyful learning of language arts.

Enthusiasm is contagious. If you love the content you teach, students will catch that passion. If you haven't already read the work of Donald Graves (e.g., *Writing: Teachers & Children at Work*, 1983), you should! His legacy is one of bringing joy to being a writer. Get excited about the writing your students do, and they will reciprocate with writing that can amaze you. Our enthusiasm makes students want to write, rather than feeling required to write. Share your own writing with students to kick-start the enthusiasm. I often read students a story about my grandfather's name-saint day (an Italian celebration) and the ice cream store in Akron, Ohio, we went to each August.

Sharing my personal writing encourages my students to be a bit more daring and to write and share, too.

Content counts. Choose the most interesting content, find the most engaging activities, and get interactions going between students. The Common Core State Standards (CCSS; National Governors Association Center for Best Practices, Council of Chief State School Officers, 2010) may tell us what students should be able to do, but only we can choose the journey. For instance, the standards state, "Write narratives to develop real or imagined experiences or events using effective technique, descriptive details, and clear event sequences" (p. 20). Ask students to take flight, hover above a favorite place (their room, Grandma's backyard, a "fun" family destination), and draw and label a map. From there they begin to write descriptive phrases that come to mind about events at that location. Students can share their maps and talk about the experiences and events. Often, new words and phrases come to mind as they talk about the map's meaning. Finally, they draft a narrative of their experiences at this favorite location. The map allows memories to flood back as words and phrases, thus encouraging even the most reluctant writer to get involved in the process.

Humans are storytellers. Find ways to weave a story into your teaching. Maybe a story is the hook at the beginning of your lesson that captures the students' attention. Remind students that their first attempt should not be their only attempt; J. K. Rowling received 12 rejections before Bloomsbury, a London publisher, agreed to publish *Harry Potter and the Philosopher's Stone* (1997; later published in the United States by Scholastic as *Harry Potter and the Sorcerer's Stone*). Tell students the story behind the comma: One of the first punctuation marks (dating back to the third century), it originally indicated the amount of breath one should take while reciting a text aloud; the word itself originates from Greek, meaning "piece cut off." Telling students a story can make a lasting impression—in this case, it can help them determine when to use a comma.

Challenge students appropriately. If you challenge students without overwhelming their learning ability, they will want to extend what you do in class. The writing they do at home, the words they look up because they are curious, and the visual representations they create as they learn new vocabulary are all self-initiated ways learning can continue beyond the four walls of your classroom.

Invite students to continue the conversation. What might students want to dive into, now that you have whetted their appetite? A classroom newspaper or blog? A word history tree? A vocabulary word wall or student-created version of a dictionary? Ask them to help make the decision, let them take ownership, and you have invited them into joyful learning.

Overview

In Chapter 1, I define what *joyful learning* means to me and provide a framework for achieving joyful learning in the classroom. This chapter presents some of the research about how and why we must engage students in their learning. Passive learning can bore or frustrate students, causing them to disengage from learning. Instead, joyful learning offers the beginning sparks to help students invest in their classroom.

In Chapter 2, I discuss how to evaluate the five elements of learning: the learner, the teacher, text and materials, assessments, and schoolwide configurations (Opitz & Ford, 2014). The reflections and assessment tools provided in this chapter will help guide instructional practice to improve student engagement and maximize the benefits of joyful learning. This evaluation is guided by three overarching questions:

- Do learners think they can succeed?
- Why do learners want to succeed?
- Do learners know what they need to succeed?

During this evaluation, we also must consider how well we are engaging students in learning and using language arts. That means we must examine our own use of the six areas of English language arts: reading, writing, speaking, listening, viewing, and visual representation.

Chapter 3 is all about how to implement the joyful learning framework in the English language arts classroom. In this chapter, I suggest some activities and strategies to engage elementary, middle, and high school learners. The strategies are framed around the five key areas in which we as teachers can promote joyful learning: school community, physical (classroom) environment, whole-group instruction, small-group instruction, and individual instruction (Opitz & Ford, 2014).

Chapter 4 brings to light some of the contemporary issues that might be lurking in the back of your mind as you read the first three chapters. How does joyful learning address the Common Core State Standards? How do we meet the needs of diverse learners, including English language learners (ELLs)? Can we meet the demands of assessments, address achievement gaps, and still keep the joy in learning?

Of these questions, one that resonates with many teachers is how to connect with diverse students, particularly ELLs. Throughout this book, I include teaching tips from Lindsey Moses, Arizona State University, that highlight how the content best connects with diverse learners, to support teachers in succeeding in creating a joyful learning classroom.

CHAPTER 1

Understanding Joyful Learning in the English Language Arts

Students need to be excited about and invested in any activity we bring to our teaching—and their learning. Investment and excitement are the essence of the joyful learning philosophy: "acquiring knowledge or skills in ways that cause pleasure and happiness" (Opitz & Ford, 2014, p. 10). Language arts encompass written (reading, writing), oral (speaking, listening), and visual (viewing, visual representation) skills—the key word in this content area is *language* (see Figure 1.1). Everything we do in life is touched by language, so whether it is delivering it or receiving it, we all must be proficient language users if we are to succeed. The joyful learning framework provides a structure within which we can motivate and engage students in the English language arts classroom.

What Is Joyful Learning?

Will Hobbs (2004) captured what we should aim for as we plan our language arts lessons, while seeking to establish a joyful learning environment: "The brain remembers what the heart cares about." In *Engaging Minds in the Classroom* (2014), Opitz and Ford discussed different motivators for students and how these influence classroom instruction (see Figure 1.2). If we choose lessons that engage and inspire our students, not only will they care about their learning, but we will also have made a lasting difference in their language arts

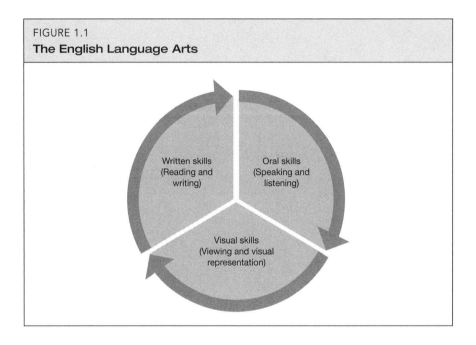

FIGURE 1.1
The English Language Arts

Written skills
(Reading and
writing)

Oral skills
(Speaking and
listening)

Visual skills
(Viewing and visual
representation)

skills. I believe that teachers can transform their classrooms into contexts that engage all students in all areas of language arts—reading, writing, speaking, listening, viewing, and visual representation.

The joyful learning framework shown in Figure 1.3 (p. 9) was devised by Mike Opitz and Mike Ford (2014) and comprises five motivational generalizations, five factors we can assess and evaluate when creating a joyful learning environment, and five areas in which we can promote learning. The joyful learning framework is based on both research and professional experience and has several attributes:

1. It capitalizes on what we know about how to best motivate students. The joyful learning framework is based upon motivating and engaging students. Graves and Watts-Taffe maintained that "getting students interested in and excited about words is a crucial component of effective literacy programs" (2008, p. 185). Murphy (2012) noted that an essential aspect of classrooms that motivate readers is giving students autonomy in making choices. When students observe their teachers engaged in these same literacy acts, they "quickly want to experience the same sense of joy" (Murphy, 2012,

FIGURE 1.2
Generalizations About Motivation, and Instructional Implications

Generalization	Description	Instructional Implication
Adaptive self-efficacy and competence beliefs motivate students.	*Self-efficacy* focuses on judgment about one's ability to successfully perform a general task ("I'm good at math") or a specific given task ("I'm very good at solving story problems"). *Competence* beliefs focus on how well a person expects to perform ("I can do this").	• Provide clear and accurate feedback regarding self-efficacy and competence, and focus on students' developing competence, expertise, and skill. • Design tasks that challenge students yet provide opportunities for success. • Involve students in monitoring their progress and growth so they can discover insights about themselves as learners.
Adaptive attributions and control beliefs motivate students.	*Attributions* and *control beliefs* are beliefs about what might cause success or failure with a given task and the degree of control one has over attaining the learning at hand. For example, "If I think deeper about this and make a greater effort, I will be able to do this" versus "I'm not as lucky as my friend who got this right."	• Provide feedback that emphasizes learning process, including the importance of effort, strategies, and self-control. • Provide strategy instruction that goes beyond declarative knowledge (what) and includes procedural (how) and conditional (why and when) knowledge as well. • Use language that focuses on controllable aspects of learning (effort, ways of thinking, strategy knowledge) and redirect language that focuses on uncontrollable aspects (luck, genes, other people's behavior). • Share examples of how "failure" is a natural part of the ultimate successful efforts. Let learners know "if at first you don't succeed, join the club!"
Higher levels of interest and intrinsic motivation motivate students.	*Value* is the importance that an individual associates with a task. *Intrinsic value* (see Wigfield & Eccles, 2002) is the enjoyment or interest the learner experiences when completing a given activity ("I can't wait to find the time so I can finish reading the next book in this series").	• Use assessment surveys that allow for insights about and across students in terms of their interests in topics, learning methods, and materials. • Provide stimulating and interesting activities that incorporate many different materials. • Provide a variety of activities, some of which are unique. • Provide content and tasks that are meaningful to students. • Show interest and involvement in the content and activities. • Allow for choice in the selection of activities, content, and materials.

(continued on next page)

FIGURE 1.2

Generalizations About Motivation, and Instructional Implications (continued)

Generalization	Description	Instructional Implication
Higher levels of value motivate students.	Other forms of value are attainment, utility, and cost (Wigfield & Eccles, 2002). *Attainment* is the importance the learner attaches to doing well on the task. *Utility* is how useful the task is to achieving a future goal ("I want to do well on this essay because I want to post it on the school website"). *Cost* is perception of the activity in terms of time and effort ("This will be a helpful way to review and it won't take a bunch of time").	• Use assessment surveys that allow for insights about and across students in terms of short-term goals, long-term goals, and current behaviors related to school work. • Provide tasks, material, and activities that are relevant and useful to students and allow for some personal identification. • Discuss with students the importance and utility of the content they are learning and the activities they complete. Help them understand why they are doing what they are doing.
Goals motivate and direct students.	*Goal content*, which focuses on establishing something to attain, and *goal orientation*, which focuses on the purpose or reason for engaging in an activity, are two important parts to consider when thinking about goals. *Mastery goal orientation* encourages students to approach the task in order to learn it well and gain new competence. *Performance goal orientation* leads one to demonstrate ability for others to seek reward or recognition (Rueda, 2011).	• Use organizational and management structures that encourage personal and social responsibility including the setting of personal and classwide goals. • Provide a safe, comfortable, and predictable environment. • Use cooperative and collaborative groups to afford students with opportunities to attain both social and academic goals. • Discuss with students the importance of mastering learning and understanding course and lesson content. • Use task, reward, and evaluation structures that promote mastery, learning, effort, progress, and self-improvement standards and deemphasize social comparison or norm-referenced standards.

Source: Generalizations adapted from Pintrich, 2002. © 2014 ASCD. Reprinted with permission from *Engaging Minds in the Classroom: The Surprising Power of Joy* by M. Opitz and M. Ford pp. 12–13.

FIGURE 1.3
Joyful Learning Framework

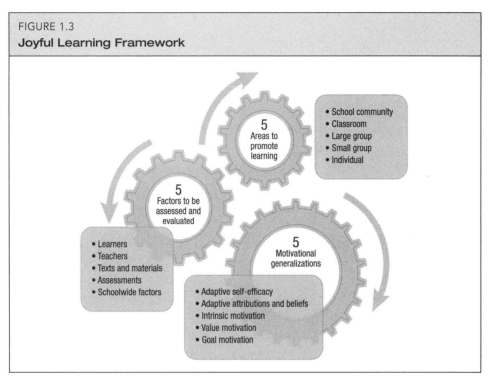

Source: © 2014 ASCD. Reprinted with permission from *Engaging Minds in the Classroom: The Surprising Power of Joy* by M. Opitz and M. Ford, p. 14.

p. 326). Students are motivated to participate when we create learning spaces in which they can feel successful.

2. It builds on what we know about student engagement. Language arts do not occur in a vacuum; we must take into account and plan for the social nature of literacy. Dockter, Haug, and Lewis (2010) believed such engagement can be achieved by allowing students to build their own understandings and to collaborate in meaningful ways, including authentic audiences and consequences, and encouraging critical and creative thinking through a high degree of rigor

Vocabulary negotiation through discussion with the teacher or peers has been shown to provide positive conditions for English language learners by including interest, understanding, repetition, deliberate attention, and generative use (Nation, 2005).

Initially, viewing and visual representation may be the language arts used most frequently by ELLs for communication. Not forcing the use of other language arts before they are ready allows them to engage with the content and their peers.

(p. 419). In this way, students naturally use language arts and see how they are applied in the world, not just applied in school.

3. It enables us to focus on the whole child. What we do in language arts ultimately reaches beyond our classrooms. Clarke and Whitney (2009) suggested that teachers find ways to connect what students read and write in the classroom to the real world. For instance, selecting texts with multiple perspectives and giving students the opportunity to read and discuss texts, create visual representations, engage in readers' theater, complete graphic organizers, write journal entries, and listen to others are all part of language arts. Teachers also can make content more comprehensible through repeated readings and scaffolded literacy activities and interactions. Finding ways to engage the whole child helps students develop "a better understanding of others, a greater appreciation of diversity, and an awareness of how to live in a globalized world" (Clarke & Whitney, 2009, p. 534).

4. It acknowledges that the learner is influenced by the contexts in which learning takes place. Social media and digital literacies are "fundamentally changing the ways in which youth today read, write, and communicate" (Sweeny, 2010, p. 121). Cunningham and Allington reminded us that "to create powerful classroom environments in which all children learn to read and write, teachers need to be concerned with models, materials, and motivation" (1999, p. 45). Designing classroom instruction that incorporates audio, video, and nontraditional texts (e.g., graphic novels, Twitter, blogs) helps students engage with different literacies and with real-world language.

There are many ways to use audio, video, and other digital resources to enhance ELL language acquisition, such as audio books, videos with closed captioning or subtitles, vocabulary and language games, and text-to-speech translation.

Defining Joyful Learning in Language Arts

Do your students love to write? Do your students think they are outstanding spellers? Do they love to present before a group? How well do they listen? When viewing an advertisement or listening to a campaign speech, do your students go beyond the surface and analyze how it makes them think and feel? Although joyful learning in language arts embraces all of these situations, most of us have preferences. Some people like to write e-mail messages, but not journal entries. Others like to talk in small groups, especially with people they know and are comfortable with, but quail at the thought of giving a speech before a large audience. Still others are happy to buy a product just because it is advertised with a catchy jingle. As adults, we all put qualifiers on our "love" of any of the language arts. Do your students do the same?

Many years ago, Robert Fulghum mused on the idea that as kindergarteners we think we can do anything (1991). Dance? YES! Sing? YES! Draw? YES! But ask a group of college students what they can do and suddenly they offer qualifiers: they "only play piano . . . only draw horses . . . only sing in the shower. . . . What happened to YES! of course I can?" (pp. 226–227). Indeed, what happened to confidence, engagement, and participation? What happened to joy? How did teaching become separated from joyful learning?

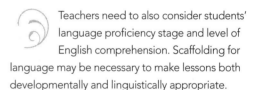

Teachers need to also consider students' language proficiency stage and level of English comprehension. Scaffolding for language may be necessary to make lessons both developmentally and linguistically appropriate.

William Louden and his colleagues (2005) grouped effective literacy teaching practices into six dimensions: participation, knowledge, orchestration, support, differentiation, and respect. Each dimension encompasses a number of characteristics. For our purposes, participation has great influence on the type of literacy skills our students acquire, and comprises:

• Attention: Our students must be focused on the learning task before them. Are the materials we ask them to use student centered? Do our students stay focused on the writing or listening task? Too long at any single task or activity can make attention slip, so it is important to create language arts lessons that are developmentally appropriate and at the right challenge level (without being frustrating or boring).

• Engagement: When a task or topic is fascinating, learning is a natural outcome. Are we finding ways to pique curiosity and keep students engaged? Do students find their own ways to become absorbed in a task (perhaps by varying the "means" to get to the "end")? Helping students make their own decisions and giving them a measure of autonomy leads to students having a vested interest in an activity and can increase engagement (Pink, 2009).

• Stimulation: Our students need a reason to engage. Is there a hook to the lesson (e.g., costumes, music, an out-of-the-ordinary event or statement) that you can use to catch their attention? Do you as the teacher convey your own enthusiasm for the lesson? If the teacher is bored, students will be, too.

• Pleasure: Humans are drawn to pleasure and tend to avoid pain. How do we make writing a pleasurable experience for the student who dislikes it? Can we find ways to transcend the worksheet, essay, or report approach? Again, incorporating autonomy by allowing students to play to their strengths can increase engagement. Do our lessons make real-life connections for students? For example, postgame interviews with sports figures or a politician's impromptu press conference can illustrate the importance of oral skills.

• Consistency: Routines help us feel safe. Does your classroom structure give confidence to your students without limiting the possibilities? Writing workshops can have a skeletal framework while leaving open the type of writing a student can do. Time to speak can be carved out each day, with a variation on the type of speaking (and listening) we do.

ELLs need scheduled time to interact and converse in English. This provides opportunities to further develop their basic interpersonal communicative skills and cognitive academic language proficiency.

Freebody (2005) has noted that

Effective teachers created energetic and exciting classrooms, in which pleasure in literacy learning was evident, as they expressed their own personal pleasure in learning tasks, stimulated suspense and antic-ipation of joyful learning, and generally communicated their plea-sure in children's work. This creation of pleasure in their classrooms encouraged children to participate, sustain their efforts and remain on task. (p. 201)

Such classrooms are a joy for teachers *and* students.

In the coming chapters, learn how we can engage students and lead them toward joyful learning. In the next chapter, explore how to evaluate the five factors of learning (learners, teachers, texts and materials, assessments, and schoolwide configurations) to ensure that they are conducive to engage-ment, motivation, and joyful learning.

CHAPTER 2

Assessing and Evaluating Joyful Learning

On a recent trip to a state park in California, I learned facts about redwoods that made my language arts "joy meter" go off. The guide led us through a maze of paths until we reached a giant redwood he called the "grandmother tree." The estimated age of the grandmother tree is 2,000 years, and it would take 17 people holding hands to encircle it. On our return hike, the guide stopped at a ring of redwoods—all perfectly straight, tall, and spaced in a perfect circle. He told us these trees had sprouted from the burls on the roots of an older tree. These trees grew interconnected to each other. I thought, "Well, there you go—those trees are like language arts. Although each stands alone, they are all linked together by a common starting point and continue to be interconnected to each other."

Although each tree (or language art) stands alone, it really does not. All the language arts rely on each other, and they are all related to something larger: the use of our language. This thought process also made me think about how we can best help our students see and value this interconnectivity. Writing helps us to express our ideas; being able to spell helps others to read our writings and understand our ideas. Listening often opens worlds we cannot access as a reader, whereas speaking gives voice to our thoughts. Viewing and visual representation provide a different format for our ideas and thoughts. To help our students see this interconnectivity, we must teach language arts in a way that shows how they are interconnected in our literate lives.

In addition to conveying the holistic nature of language arts to our students, we need to situate this education within the joyful learning framework. Opitz and Ford (2014) suggested conducting a systematic assessment of key elements within the learning environment that can help teachers target specific concerns or help guide instruction. The five elements we must evaluate include the learner, ourselves as teachers, the texts and materials we use for the class, the standardized assessments that help us gauge learning and student progress, and schoolwide configurations. Assessing each of these elements is essential to establishing a joyful learning classroom environment.

Assessing and Evaluating Learners

Understanding the ways our students use literacy is critical if we are to enhance their use of all language processes. What is the extent of their academic and social vocabularies? How well do they write and express their ideas? Do they spell grade-level words conventionally, and use appropriate grammar and syntax? How well do they use listening to learn and to help them explore topics in new ways? These are a few of the many questions we need to ask (and answer) to help us better understand our students. Understanding what students think they can do, want to do, and know what they need to do to succeed (Opitz & Ford, 2014) enables us to plan for joyful language instruction and learning.

Consider an experience I had in a 5th grade classroom. One student brought his writing to me, wanting to know what other information he should include. He had written *My cat had a harditak*. Behind him stood another student holding her story, with a sentence saying that she needed a *flicewater*. These two students showed me how their knowledge of vocabulary and their listening abilities (*heart attack* and *fly swatter*) had influenced their writing. They were excited to be writing self-selected stories, but they knew that they needed some guidance in understanding the reader's perspective. They brought something to the language arts table, and I could use what they already knew to extend their understanding.

When assessing learners, using the three broad areas of language arts discussed in Chapter 1—written skills, oral skills, and visual skills—makes the

FIGURES 2.1 Evaluating Learners' Language Arts Skills	
Written skills (reading and writing)	• Do they read at an instructional grade level that gives them access to a variety of texts? • Do they comprehend the texts they read? • Can they think critically about what they read? • Can they write texts of varying genres? • Do they use a wide range of vocabulary to express their ideas? • Can they independently review and revise their writing?
Oral skills (speaking and listening)	• Can they organize their thinking in ways to verbally present their ideas? • Do they have a range of speaking skills useful in large and small groups? • Can they participate in the logical sequence of a "give and take" conversation? • Can they process and respond to a text that is presented to them through a read-aloud or audio book? • Can they effectively summarize main points presented by a speaker? • Can they comprehend content that is above their reading level, but at their level of intellectual capacity?
Visual skills (viewing and visual representation)	• Can they analyze and interpret images they view? • Can they utilize a variety of media to enhance their understanding of content? • Can they evaluate the purpose of the images they view? • Can they analyze and interpret visual representations such as graphs, timelines, and organizers? • Can they create visual representations of content? • Can they demonstrate understanding by using multiple sign systems?

process manageable and practical; it also enables us to see the interconnectedness of our students' knowledge (see Figure 2.1).

Written Skills (Reading and Writing)

Tools such as the Authentic Text Reading Record (Opitz, Ford, & Erekson, 2011) can be used to record data relating to students' accuracy, reading level, and comprehension; the goal of any assessment is to reveal student needs that will help shape the classroom teacher's response.

• Can students with similar needs be grouped for minilessons to improve reading skills? (See Chapter 3 section on small-group instruction.)

• Do specific skills need to be targeted for some students, as observed in this reading record? This may guide individual instruction (see Chapter 3).

• Are there commonalities across all students in class? Commonalities can help shape whole-group instruction (see Chapter 3).

Students who seem to exhibit weaknesses in grade-level vocabulary might benefit from learning to use vocabulary flags. Younger students can use a chart to record what they think a word means and then record the dictionary definition as a means of self-assessment. Older students can highlight words and note the definition in the margin as a review tool. For all ages, checking to see if there are common challenges can dictate classroom response (e.g., preteaching vocabulary, reading passages aloud, highlighting or discussing challenging terms).

Use writing assessments to identify students' strengths in spelling, in using descriptive words, and in organizing their thoughts into a coherent piece of writing. Then, identify what seems to be absent from a student's repertoire of strategies. Where does the student seem to get frustrated? After reviewing students' writing samples, you should be able to identify the most important issues to attend to instructionally, both for individual students and the class as a whole. Similarly, students can conduct writing self-assessments that include both prewriting (what are the main points, who is the audience, what terms and words are appropriate) and postwriting components (effectiveness of points, vocabulary, and descriptive writing; whether the piece was appropriate for intended audience). Student self-assessments can guide teacher–student conferences in which students are able to identify areas in which their skills can be improved.

Oral Skills (Speaking and Listening)

Use charts to record your observations of conversations in which your students participate, in whole-group and small-group instruction. For younger students, it can be helpful to use Halliday's language functions (1975) to identify types of language developing speakers are using.

- Do students lack a specific type of language use? If so, what group experience could you plan to encourage use of that type of language?
- Do specific students lack a specific type of language use? If so, what experiences could you plan for these students to encourage use of that type of language?

For older students, observing their participation in small-group activities such as book circles (see Chapter 3) or group projects can help you develop material to support their oral skills. Observing student interactions and class participation also can help direct classroom instruction. When observing students in small-group instruction and in whole-group instruction, ask

- Would minilessons improve student understanding of a particular part of the reading?
- Do students need notes or guidelines to support their participation?
- When students participate in the discussion, can they convey their ideas and share in the conversation?

When assessing students' listening skills, forms such as Opitz and Zbaracki's Listening Level Checklist (2004) can assist in identifying students' discriminative, precise, strategic, critical, and appreciative listening. Reviewing the results of listening skills assessments can help you select a listening level that best fits different classroom activities, help you identify experiences to provide students help in developing various levels of listening, and guide discussion with students about strengths and weaknesses.

Visual Skills (Viewing and Visual Representation)

Students are growing up in a society that is rife with visual images. They are exposed to a variety of images on their smartphones, tablets, computers, and televisions that they need to be able to decipher and interpret. Understanding how students interpret and design visual messages is essential to creating effective English language arts lessons that help students learn how to interpret visual messages and to create visual representations of their own ideas.

In assessing students' visual skills, provide a range of age-appropriate images in whole-group and small-group settings and discuss the emotions or ideas that students derive from those images. Use the information from these activities to determine:

- What types of viewing do the students need more experiences in?
- What activities should you plan to expand viewing skills?

Graphic organizers, mind maps, charts, graphs, and other visual tools can help students both organize their ideas and explain them to others. Assessing students' abilities to interpret and present information visually can be conducted as a whole-group activity, where the teacher models creating (or interpreting) a graphic organizer or mind map and students contribute or suggest information to include. Such an activity will allow you to assess how well students contribute to or understand the information depicted, and can lead to developing additional activities to strengthen competence in this skill area. Showing students how to use charts and graphs to self-assess can also support their visual representation skills.

As Opitz and Ford noted in *Engaging Minds in the Classroom* (2014), "although the assessment and evaluation begins with a focus on the learner, it cannot end there. Affective outcomes are neither inherent to nor solely the responsibility of the learner" (pp. 26–30). As part of the process of establishing a joyful learning environment, we need to assess the teacher, texts and materials, assessments, and schoolwide configurations, in addition to evaluating learners. All of these elements, like the six areas of language arts, are interrelated.

 Many ELLs rely on their visual skills in the beginning stages of language acquisition. Encourage the development and use of these skills to support students in developing their written and oral skills..

Evaluating Ourselves as Teachers

Thinking about how well our students do in language arts requires us to consider our own skills in reading, writing, speaking, listening, viewing, and in visually representing information. Do we find joy in using the language arts in our everyday lives? Researchers point to the teacher as an influential model in reading (Methe & Hintze, 2003) and writing (Grainger, 2005); there is "a strong functional relationship between on-task reading behavior and teacher modeling" (Methe & Hintze, 2003, p. 620). If we participate in and value reading, we send a clear message to our students, making it more likely that they will follow our lead. To teach writing effectively we must move "from being mere instructors in the classroom to informed facilitators and fellow writers" (Grainger, 2005, p. 86). Participating in literate acts confirms for our students that these are important skills, whether it is showing them that we enjoy writing in our journals or reading books to learn something new. Therefore, as part of assessing ourselves as language arts teachers, we must ask ourselves a series of questions (see Figure 2.2).

Once we are cognizant of how we use language, we need to share our thoughts with students to make clear what we value and why these are important life skills. Simple comments such as "You know, I was reading the paper this morning and I saw this chart. . . ," "Last night on TV I saw this ad about . . . and wondered. . . ," and "I was listening to the radio on the way to school this morning. . . ." show students the connections between language arts and real life. Your comments indicate that you value these language activities and find them to be joyful.

Some key words to consider are *opportunity* and *demonstration*. Cambourne (1988) believed the acquisition of literacy is best served by several conditions of learning, one of which is demonstration. Through modeling, teachers can demonstrate both the importance of language arts skills and how joyful being confident in them can be. At the same time, we need to extend the opportunity to our students to try out these skills in a variety of ways that will lead them to their own concept of joy in learning.

Evaluating Texts and Materials

Language arts are interrelated; in our classrooms, students may listen to something and then create a written text or a visual representation of what they learned. They might create an oral presentation after viewing a website and

FIGURE 2.2 Evaluating Ourselves as Language Arts Teachers	
Written skills (reading and writing)	• Do I purposefully select a variety of texts? • What do I do to comprehend the texts I read? • Do I think critically about what I read? • Do I construct texts of varying genres? • Do I use a wide range of vocabulary to express my ideas? • Do I regularly review and revise my writing?
Oral skills (speaking and listening)	• Do I organize my thinking to verbally present my ideas? • Do I use a range of speaking skills in large and small groups? • Do I participate in the logical sequence of a "give and take" conversation? • How do I process and respond to a text that is presented through a read-aloud? • Do I effectively summarize main points presented by a speaker? • Do I seek to listen to and comprehend content at my level of intellectual capacity?
Visual skills (viewing and visual representation)	• Do I analyze and interpret images I view? • Do I utilize a variety of media to enhance my understanding of content? • Do I evaluate the purpose of the images I view? • Do I analyze and interpret visual representations such as graphs, timelines, and organizers? • Do I create visual representations of content? • Do I demonstrate understanding by using multiple sign systems?

reading the information posted there. They read books, e-books, and online texts that are full of visual images and then participate in a discussion of how those images extend and enhance the writing. We use language arts in dozens of combinations, so we need to carefully evaluate the texts and materials we use with students.

• Do classroom texts and materials reflect a grade-level range that provides all students easy access to content?

• Do materials help students develop a wide range of vocabulary to express their ideas?

• Do materials require students to process and respond through listening, either through read-alouds or recorded text?

• Do materials challenge students to comprehend content that is above their reading level, but at their level of intellectual capacity?

• Do texts and materials encourage students to use a variety of media to enhance their understanding of content?

• Do the materials help them analyze and interpret visual representations such as graphs, timelines, and organizers?

Language arts skills are essential for student success throughout the curriculum; students need to read, write, speak, listen, view, and visually represent ideas and concepts in science, social studies, and mathematics. As Donoghue (2009) noted, the discovery of content through the use of language arts creates a perfect partnership in our curriculum: "Students are enabled through their language abilities to discuss and write" (p. 83) about content. So, evaluating materials as to whether they encourage joyful learning in language arts also means assessing how well we engage students in purposeful use of those skills in other areas of the curriculum.

Evaluating Assessments

English language arts assessments measure students' skills and knowledge in each of the six areas. We need to know how well students read, write, speak, listen, view, and use visual representations, and what they need to know in order to become proficient in each area. Formative assessment combines systematic teacher observations with samples of student work. Formative assessment is one of "the most important measures of student achievement" (*Primary Sources*, 2010, p. 25); teachers "can utilize the information they collect from their assessment of student learning to make adjustments in instruction, and students can use feedback from frequent assessments to adjust their own learning strategies" (Frey & Schmitt, 2010, p. 108). We can use our observations of how students use their skills in everyday authentic applications to create lessons that will enhance their learning. For instance, in an elementary classroom, perhaps a few students do not carry over the words learned in spelling to writing tasks such as journals. A quick lesson that shows last week's spelling words and a journal entry with errors on those same words is a useful demonstration of how we learn to spell—not just for the Friday test, but also for our everyday writing. In middle or high school classrooms, assessing whether students are using appropriate vocabulary and terminology in their writing might lead to a similar modeling of how to incorporate words from foundational texts into student work.

Standardized tests "'boil down' the essence of what a student has learned" (Fresch & Wheaton, 2002, p. 48). So, which assessments should we choose? Assessments should meet the needs of your classroom and population of students, and many excellent tools are readily available (see Opitz, Ford, & Erekson, 2011). When choosing assessments, or evaluating those your school uses, consider their efficiency in assessing students in all areas of language arts.

- Do the assessments show how well students read? Do they assess students' reading fluency, comprehension, and critical thinking?

- Do the assessments require students to construct texts of varying genres and evaluate how well students met various criteria? Do they assess students' use of grade-level vocabulary in authentic ways? Do they assess students' abilities to independently review and revise their own writing?

- Do the assessments reveal how organized students' thinking is, as demonstrated in their verbally presented ideas? Are there different ways of assessing students' speaking skills in large and small groups?

- Do assessments show how effectively students summarize main points presented by a speaker or audio material? Do the assessments reveal whether students comprehend content that is above their reading level, but at their level of intellectual capacity?

- Do assessments indicate how students analyze and interpret images and how they use a variety of media? Do the assessments indicate whether students are able to analyze and interpret visual representations?

In addition to standardized assessment tools, checklists, and charts, interactive whole-class techniques such as thumbs up/thumbs down, one-minute papers, and journals can help to address these questions in manageable ways—and effectively give us a look at how well our students are progressing. Students can assess their work to provide focused feedback on their own skills and thought processes (Andrade, Wang, Du, & Akawi, 2009). Using a combination of these tools and interpreting findings can put us in a position to better understand where students are and where they need to improve as they progress to becoming more proficient.

Figure 2.3 is the result of sifting through the many different assessment tools that teachers use to assess language arts skills. Keeping assessment a joyful rather than an arduous experience was at the forefront of my mind. So, rather than provide an exhaustive list, I chose ones that are relatively easy to administer for each language art. I offer some guidance for assessment tools and strategies for student self-assessment. Many of these tools overlap, and a single assessment can certainly give a good idea of how students are using their language arts skills. You probably already use some assessments that are effective in evaluating at least some of the essential areas listed.

As Opitz and Ford noted, "*Joy* and *testing* are two words we don't often see in the same sentence" (2014, p. 33). However, when students self-assess, when you provide feedback on how well they are doing, when you nudge them on because they can do more, and they smile as they realize what they have accomplished—then you have a true indication of joy after assessment.

Evaluating Schoolwide Configurations

Every schoolwide activity should illustrate some facet of real-life use of language arts. Frank Smith (1988) told us long ago of the importance of joining the literacy club: When students "have opportunities to see what written language can do, they are encouraged and helped to do those things themselves, and they are not at risk of exclusion if they make mistakes" (p. 217). Finding ways to connect students to the real-world use of oral, written, and visual skills provides significant support for their development. Schoolwide activities will impress on students that we are all users of these skills, regardless of what we do or how old we are.

I once visited a school where the custodian came into a kindergarten classroom to read aloud a community helper book about his job. After he read, the students asked him questions and the teacher recorded the answers on chart paper. He talked about how he must carefully read repair manuals, accurately write orders for supplies, listen carefully to someone explaining a

FIGURE 2.3
Assessment of English Language Arts Skills

Language Art	Areas to Assess	Assessment Tools	Student Self-Assessment Strategies
Reading	• Fluency • Comprehension • Critical thinking • Willingness and ability to read range of texts	• Authentic Text Reading Record (Opitz, Ford, & Erekson, 2011) • Burke Reading Interview (Goodman, Watson, & Burke, 1987)	• Vocabulary flag (p. 17) • Question/answer relationship activity (Raphael & Au, 2005) • Question the Author (Beck & McKeown, 1996)
Writing	• Ability to construct texts of varying genres • Vocabulary knowledge • Ability to review and revise	• Writing sample analysis (Fresch, 2001) • Informal vocabulary inventory (Morris et al., 2011; Rasinski, 2013) • Qualitative Inventory of Word Knowledge (Schlagal, 1992)	• Writing guide • Self-assessment rubric (Romeo, 2008) • 6+1 Traits rubric (Culham, 2009)
Speaking	• Organized thinking to verbally present ideas • Speaking skills in large and small-group settings • Participation in conversation (give and take)	• Halliday's language functions (Halliday, 1975) • Oral language checklist (Ogle & Beers, 2004) • Checklist of speaking skills (Beaty, 2013)	• Book circle discussion (pp. 31–41) • Portfolio checklist (Wagner & Lilly, 1999) • Grand Conversation (Peterson & Eds, 1991)
Listening	• Response to presentation of information (read-alouds, audio) • Ability to summarize main points • Comprehension of content above reading level	• Listening level checklist (Opitz & Zbaracki, 2004) • Observational matrix (Ogle & Beers, 2004) • Interactive read-alouds (Hoyt, 2007)	• Self-assessment form for listening (Opitz & Zbaracki, 2004) • Single-point rubric (Fluckiger, 2010) • Anticipation guide (Duffelmeyer, 1994)
Viewing	• Analysis and interpretation of images • Use of media • Ability to evaluate purposes of images	• Picture viewing checklist • Wordless picture book viewing (Jalongo, Dragich, Conrad, & Zhang, 2002) • Clever Cloze (Commonwealth of Australia, 2002b)	• Post–picture viewing self-assessment • Question the Painter (Williams, 2007) • Codes of Visual Text (Commonwealth of Australia, 2002a)

(continued on next page)

| FIGURE 2.3 |||||
| **Assessment of English Language Arts Skills** *(continued)* |||||

Language Art	Areas to Assess	Assessment Tools	Student Self-Assessment Strategies
Visual representation	• Analysis and interpretation of images (graphic organizers, mind maps, charts and graphs) • Ability to create images • Understanding of multiple sign systems	• Graphic organizer (e.g., KWHL, Stead, 2006; KWL, Ogle, 1986) • Electronic scrapbook (Hancock, 2007)	• Graphic organizer (e.g., What I Understand, I-Chart, Hoffman, 1992) • Sketch to stretch (Harste & Burke, 1988) • Tableaux (Tortello, 2004)

problem, explain to someone what needs to be repaired, understand a visual representation of the plumbing in the cafeteria, and draw a map of wiring that was problematic. In that short presentation he effectively showed how he used language arts and in turn encouraged students to think about what they do that might be similar to what he described.

Another school I visited adopted a schoolwide time for sustained silent reading. At a certain point every week everyone in the school—no matter who you were (even if a visitor)—stopped and read for 15 minutes. Other schools—elementary, middle, and high school—participate in "one school, one book" activities (see http://www.onemorepagebooks.com/educatorsandlibrarians/oneschoolonebook.html), which, like sustained silent reading, send a powerful message to students that adults find reading to be a joyful endeavor. The point of these types of activities is to impress on students that every adult uses the skills they are learning.

In assessing schoolwide configurations, you are seeking to establish whether the personnel in your school demonstrate that they read a range of materials and think critically about them, use vocabulary in authentic ways, use a range of speaking skills, make an effort to comprehend "difficult" content, and are able to interpret and present ideas in a variety of ways. Demonstrating these skills across the curriculum emphasizes for students that they are part of a community of learners. Elementary school physical education teachers or middle or high school health teachers might include writing activities that "promote the knowledge and attitudes essential to the goal of maintaining a healthy and fit lifestyle" (Behrman, 2004, p. 26). Science teachers can use graphic organizers, journals, and post-experiment writing to help students "provide evidence and reasoning to back up their claims" (Grymonpré, Cohn, & Solomon, 2012, p. 24). In social studies classes, students can participate in critical reading and in debating the messages they receive through various media, as part of their "roles as citizens in a democracy" (Jacobowitz & Sudol, 2010, p. 62). The idea we must embrace is showing students that we are, indeed, a community of language arts users engaged in joyful learning.

Moving Forward in the English Language Arts

To move forward, we must look back. What do we already do that ensures joyful learning in language arts? Those are the practices we want to continue. In what areas do we need to improve? Assessing each of the five elements that influence joyful learning gives us a guide for implementing the framework. In the next chapter you'll find strategies that will infuse joy into your teaching and student learning. The hope is that each strategy will give you a renewed joy in teaching language arts.

CHAPTER 3

Implementing Joyful Learning

As educators, we strive to create an environment in which students can be active, motivated learners, engaged and invested in the work they do. One way to achieve this is to weave language arts throughout instruction to serve the entire curriculum. We have multiple opportunities to read, write, listen, speak, view, and visually represent information in all content areas. Rather than solitary language arts instruction, engaging, joyful learning experiences should help students learn language arts and allow them to use language arts to engage with meaningful learning activities. In this chapter, we will consider several strategies for fostering enthusiasm and joy in the classroom to keep students motivated, engaged, and invested in their learning.

One of the essential characteristics of successful instructional programs for ELLs is meaningful, cooperative learning interactions between teachers and pupils (Genesee, Lindholm-Leary, Saunders, & Christian, 2005).

Strategies for Joyful Learning

In *Engaging Minds in the Classroom*, Opitz and Ford (2014) presented a framework for promoting joyful learning that incorporates efforts in five learning environments and configurations: the school community, the physical

FIGURE 3.1

Coordinating Learning Environments with Supportive Activities

Learning environment/ configuration	Rationale	Sample activity	Language arts used
Schoolwide community	Create a school climate that enhances learning	Career Day	Listening, speaking, writing
		Night at the Museum	Reading, writing, speaking, listening, viewing
Classroom environment	Set the stage	Learning Centers	Reading, writing, speaking, listening, viewing, using visual representation
		Book Jacket Design	Reading, writing, viewing, using visual representation, listening, speaking
Whole-group instruction	Create a community of learners	News at Six	Reading, writing, speaking, listening, viewing, using visual representation
		Poetry Machine	Reading, writing, viewing, speaking, listening
Small-group instruction	Promote social interaction	Book Circles	Reading, writing, listening, speaking
		Movie Critics	Viewing, listening, speaking, writing
Individual instruction	Allow choice and interest	What's My History?	Reading, speaking, listening
		Classified Information	Reading, writing, speaking

(classroom) environment, whole-group instruction, small-group instruction, and individual instruction. They provided a rationale for addressing each one, described structures to guide planning and implementing improvements, and offered sample instructional activities to exploit the advantages of each environment and configuration. In this chapter, I follow the same approach in organizing language arts learning activities (see Figure 3.1). In selecting learning activities to showcase in this chapter, I followed Opitz and Ford's suggestion of identifying activities that easily

- Cross content areas and grade levels;
- Incorporate readily available resources;
- Fit into existing schoolwide and classroom routines; and
- Lead to both affective (joyful) and cognitive (learning) outcomes.

My overriding goal is to provide strategies that enable students to find real joy in developing and using their language skills in novel ways.

School Community

A century ago, John Dewey acknowledged just how important the community of a school is: "The school must itself be a community life . . . where there is give and take in the building up of a common experience" (1916, p. 358). Seeing how language arts are used by members of our communities—at home and at school—helps establish purpose to the learning students will do. If they can see how others use language arts in real life, they will understand that these skills are not just something we learn in school, but something we use throughout our lifetime. Whatley and Canalis suggested that creating "community is the first step teachers at all levels can take to help students realize their personal and academic potential as well as learn about how people live and work together" (2002, p. 487). Creating activities that draw the community into our classroom provides the link of school and real life.

Let's return to the story in Chapter 2 about the custodian who visited the kindergarten classroom. Reading a book about his job, and discussing with students how he used different skills, is a good example of a community member demonstrating the joy in learning and using language arts. This idea can be the basis for an activity that not only incorporates language arts activities but

Be sure to include aspects of the community that are representative of your classroom population. Identifying ELLs in the community can help students understand their personal and academic potential as bilingual speakers..

also introduces students to members of their school and wider community and incorporates career education.

Career Day. During Career Day, members of the school and surrounding community not only interact with students in discussing their jobs but also demonstrate the use of language arts in life. The format can be as simple as having different members of the school community (bus driver, custodian, cafeteria worker, school psychologist, mail carrier) spend some time with younger students, reading a book aloud and answering questions. Or think outside the box about giving students a wide vision of careers. Depending on the level of your students, you could coordinate a career fair that is attended by several classes or the whole school, similar to a college fair. Your local chamber of commerce is a resource for connecting with local business owners (e.g., shop owner, factory plant manager, landscaper, dog trainer, allergist, moving company scheduler, bowling alley owner, fitness instructor). Develop questions with student input prior to the presentation and seek ways to connect speakers to content studies (e.g., landscaper could connect to science and talk specifically about environmental concerns in the area; moving company representative could provide geography connections by presenting a map on company locations and movement; fitness instructor could connect to physical education and discuss age-appropriate ways to stay fit). Local professional organizations might be able to provide you with names of individuals interested in mentoring or interacting with students, and you could approach parents through the school's PTA or PTO for support as well. As a follow-up activity, students could complete oral or written reports about different careers, or conduct additional research to explore fields of interest or topics raised by the speakers.

Including a bilingual professional would allow students to create questions about literacy, content, and use of multiple languages, as well as build community and greater understanding among ELLs and native English speakers.

Night at the Museum. This activity brings families and school staff together. Through personal sharing, students learn more about others in their community and are actively engaged in using their language arts skills. Each school staff member and each school family selects and displays an artifact that represents something important to them, accompanied by an index card that explains the significance of the artifact to the staff member or family. At Night at the Museum, families and school staff tour the displays. As a follow-up activity, ask students to reflect on their own displays and also what they learned about someone else. Which artifact surprised them? What was something really interesting that they learned about someone? The community feeling developed through this night can have long-range effects by creating new connections among students and staff. Students also see real purposes of reading, writing, viewing, and discussing in this community event.

Seeing their family artifacts represented among the school community can be empowering for ELLs, and providing descriptor cards in advance allows the family time to prepare for successful interactions in English.

The format can be altered for middle and high school students; perhaps challenge them to select artifacts that represent something in their lives that their fellow students don't know about them. Later, have students use their own artifact or someone else's as inspiration for a short writing activity. Another option for middle or high school is to create a video or slide show that teachers throughout the school can show and discuss, or to use the artifacts as a guessing game to match the artifact to the student or staff member.

Classroom Environment

Every theater director understands the importance of setting the stage. As teachers, how we construct our classrooms can invite students into becoming independent, successful language arts users or leave them feeling unwelcome.

Creating a Community of Learners

All students deserve to be offered numerous opportunities to engage in reading, writing, listening, speaking, viewing, and using visual representation. In addition, as Pohan noted, "every lesson we teach is potentially an opportunity to prepare our students for active and productive participation in a diverse and democratic society" (2000, p. 28). Surrounding all students with motivating and engaging ways to use their skills brings a purposeful focus to our classrooms.

Learning Centers. Learning centers provide opportunities for students to review content, extend beyond content already taught, or dive into new content. When designing a learning center, here are some considerations to help ensure successful implementation.

1. Ensure that the activities are focused on individual or small-group cooperative (no more than five or six students) work.

2. Make the activities "self-checking" to encourage independence and flow in student work.

3. Prepare games (e.g., responding to quiz cards or challenges, acting, solving a puzzle or mystery) to help students apply content-area information.

4. Adapt materials that you already have, perhaps those lurking in closets or file drawers that you never seem to get to teach. Materials do not have to be fancy or expensive.

5. Supply storage for work in the form of a file box or crate. Label a folder for each student where he or she can store materials, whether the activity is complete or not. A storage system makes it easy for students to pick up where they left off the day or week before—and avoids the excuses of having left materials at home or in the locker.

6. Encourage a feeling of community by scheduling sharing time. Pick time on a Friday or a lull in the day to have students share with their classmates what they have accomplished in the centers. Students feel joy and pride in sharing their successes, and these experiences build community by providing for natural interaction—and may inspire interest in different activities.

Figure 3.2, p. 34, suggests a variety of activities for learning centers that cover the six language arts areas and cross grade levels.

FIGURE 3.2
Learning Center Ideas Across Grade Levels

Language Art	Elementary School	Middle School	High School
Reading	Free choice at library shelf. Checklist to record choices and encourage selection of different genres.	Choice of three or four titles on similar themes. Later, small discussion groups meet to discuss and reflect on the book.	Paired sets of fiction and nonfiction texts. Students self-select titles and create compare-and-contrast projects with a partner or individually.
Writing	Workshop area with paper, pencils, markers. Students are encouraged to develop storyline of choice (fiction or nonfiction).	Workshop area with variety of graphic organizers to help students prewrite. Organizers may be specific to fiction, nonfiction, and poetry.	Workshop area with materials for prewriting and organization (e.g., computer programs to convert graphic organizer to outline); additional online or textbook resources for nonfiction writing; samples of variety of poetry types.
Speaking	Picture and chapter books with recording device (tape recorder, computer). Students read book or selection aloud and then add personal comments at conclusion.	Reader's Theater scripts to read and practice aloud. Students may also create their own scripts using favorite or teacher-selected texts.	Wordless picture "books." Students create storylines to coincide with different illustrations. Students may compare and contrast their stories with each other's and original source.
Listening	Recorded storybooks. After listening, students respond by illustrating their favorite part and discussing their drawings with center partners. Older elementary students may create follow-up questions for story characters or author.	Audio book selections. Students respond after listening to a series of teacher-constructed questions or discuss with center partners.	Recorded podcasts of content-related work in other areas of the curriculum. Follow-up writing asks students to summarize what they learned or draw connections to additional content areas.
Viewing	Short videos of fiction or nonfiction storybooks. Students respond after the viewing by illustrating an interesting segment and discuss with center partners.	Videos of fiction or nonfiction books. Students respond after the viewing to a series of teacher-constructed questions or in discussion with center partners.	Video clips of content related to work in other area of the curriculum. Follow-up writing task asks students to summarize what they learned, or analyze intent of presentation.

FIGURE 3.2 Learning Center Ideas Across Grade Levels *(continued)*			
Language Art	**Elementary School**	**Middle School**	**High School**
Visual representation	Students create illustrations to enhance writing workshop story or in response to listening or viewing center activity.	Students create or search for Internet illustrations to enhance writing workshop story or in response to listening or viewing center activity.	Students create or search for Internet illustrations to enhance writing workshop story or in response to listening or viewing center activity.

Book Jacket Design. Having students design book covers is an activity that can enhance the joyful learning environment by identifying students as learners, and it also has them use all of their language arts skills. Prior to introducing the activity, review visual representation skills by showing students different book jackets or advertisements for movies and discussing the intent of the design or how the image expresses the author's purpose or the content. For the activity, students create a jacket for a book the entire class is reading, a chapter from a read-aloud, or a student-selected text. The cover design should reflect what the story is about. Middle and high school students can take this assignment further by summarizing the story on an inside flap and providing some information about the author. Students also might prepare a presentation about the book to encourage others to read it. For fiction, students should provide information about the plot and setting; for a nonfiction book, students could discuss the topic and some interesting facts. Sharing individual student projects could be similar to Night at the Museum, with students touring one another's displays, or you could schedule presentations over the course of the week and then display the covers on the classroom walls. A follow-up activity might include having a selection of the books available in learning centers or holding small-group discussions about the same book—or books with similar themes.

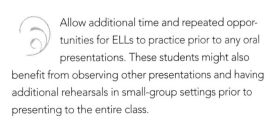 Allow additional time and repeated opportunities for ELLs to practice prior to any oral presentations. These students might also benefit from observing other presentations and having additional rehearsals in small-group settings prior to presenting to the entire class.

Whole-Group Instruction

"We are in this together" develops a feeling of camaraderie that provides companionship throughout the learning journey. Whole-group activities provide camaraderie and companionship as they enable all students to work toward the same goal. These activities do not mean that all students have to do the same work, in the same way. In fact, Carol Ann Tomlinson argued for differentiating whole-group instruction, "'shaking up' what goes on in the classroom so that students have multiple options for taking information, making sense of ideas, and expressing what they learn" (2001, p. 1). Students feel successful and empowered when they can accomplish self-selected activities. They find joy and their voice in contributing to the larger group. Effective whole-group instruction leads to students valuing both their own work and the work of their peers.

Cooperative Projects

Whole-group instruction can incorporate both individual student choice and use of specific strengths and interests, as well as cooperative learning and teamwork. Using a combination of these strategies serves to keep students engaged and reinforces the idea of the classroom as a community of learners. In language arts, it also provides an opportunity for students to make real-life connections to their learning.

News at Six. News at Six is an activity that employs all six language arts while allowing for individual choice and use of specific strengths and interests, and it is easily adapted to different age and grade levels (see Figure 3.3). The basic idea is to create a news station in your classroom, structuring the work of each department based on the grade level of your students. Younger students may need less written work and more support to do the research and writing for each role. The "news show" can be a special event during a regular school day, an evening event for families and school community, or it can be recorded and watched as a class. Groups of older students can work independently in their news department, with the class as a whole combining and creating the final show, or a group of students might take charge of editing and organizing the order of news stories. As a follow-up activity, students

FIGURE 3.3
News at Six

News Department	Student Activities		
	Elementary School	**Middle School**	**High School**
Headline news	Provide students with easy-to-read headlines. Students decide what the story is behind the headline and write the news story. Older elementary school students self-select headlines from newspapers or summarize actual news stories.	Students research a current event at school. They interview key individuals and write a story providing a factual account of the event.	Students research local, national, or international events or incidents. They write stories that provide factual information surrounding the event. Students may also develop opinion pieces on headline events.
Weather	Provide students with a weather map from a local newspaper. Students develop a report discussing upcoming weather and what clothing or outdoor activities might be appropriate. Older elementary students may use Internet weather resources.	Students research upcoming weather using print and Internet resources and create an illustrated map of school grounds. Students write text explaining and interpreting map images.	Students research and report on a specific weather event (e.g., hurricane, tornado, jet stream, warm and cold fronts). They should incorporate illustrations or images to assist listeners in understanding the topic.
Science desk	Provide students will age-appropriate nonfiction texts about a specific topic (a different book for each student in the group). Students summarize basic information and create an illustration of the topic. Older elementary students may use Internet resources to collectively explore a common science topic.	Group selects a topic of interest, or one related to current study in this content area. Students read articles, books, and online resources, then summarize in a story to inform listeners. As appropriate, students incorporate video clips to illustrate and aid listener understanding.	
Sports	Provide students with some sports scores of local teams. Based on the scores, students make up a story about the game, focusing on one team in particular and highlighting exciting events.	Students report on recent sporting events in the area (local college or professional team game, competition). Students may add video clips as appropriate.	Students report on high school sports event (team sport, club activity). Students may add video clips as appropriate.

(continued on next page)

	Student Activities		
News Department	**Elementary School**	**Middle School**	**High School**
Human interest	Students interview a school staff member. Story should include information about the person's job, why he or she likes working at the school, what skills are needed for the job, and the individual's hobbies or outside interests. Older elementary students may create a video of the interview or video montage illustrating essential facts about the person.	Students compile a story about extracurricular activities (i.e., clubs) at the school, or students' outside activities. Students may add video clips as appropriate.	Students research and report on a local or national human interest story, incorporating video clips as appropriate.

FIGURE 3.3
News at Six *(continued)*

assess both their own work and the overall impact of the news show. How well did each department present its information? What sorts of images or figurative language did groups use to enhance interest and understanding? What additional writing or images might have improved the show?

Poetry Machine. In this activity, the class creates a poem together. It's a fairly quick yet effective and fun way to introduce poetry writing, and because it can be silly, it also aids in developing a class identity.

For younger elementary school students, show students a simple image (a flower, a piece of fruit, an animal, or a landscape). Have students brainstorm descriptive words and phrases; write these on the board, overhead, or an interactive whiteboard. Then, use the phrases to create either a haiku or a rhyming poem, asking students to suggest transitional phrases and other words to help the poem flow—or help students create an acrostic using the descriptive phrases.

The same approach can be used for older students, with some adaptation. Ask students to bring in examples of effective descriptive phrases, words, or figures of speech from what they are reading in other content areas, the newspaper, or online resources, and then use the phrases to create a free verse or another type of poem depending upon the unit of study. (See National Endowment for the Humanities, n.d., for additional ideas for whole-class poetry writing.)

Small-Group Instruction

Small-group activities encourage students to work together to solve a problem, create something, or pool their knowledge about a topic. Students find joy (and fun) in these activities, which are supportive and keep everyone engaged. As Slavin and Cooper noted, "the use of such methods improves academic achievement as well as intergroup relations" (1999, p. 648). Working together, students discover and learn to value their similarities, differences, and unique abilities.

Sharing Ideas

Students' academic and noncognitive abilities both progress as a result of interacting with others. Small-group activities designed to have students discuss first and then write have resulted in marked improvement in the quality of students' work (Reznitskaya et al., 2001). In the activities I provide as examples of small-group instruction, students share and compare their opinions, collectively developing insight about the texts they read as well as their overall language arts skills.

Book Circles. Book circle discussions help students gain a greater understanding of texts, as well as provide teachers with a way to assess students' oral skills (see Chapter 2). One way to enhance student participation in book circles is to provide students with a graphic organizer of guided questions for their reading (see Figure 3.4). Another approach to book circles, in the elementary grades, is to assign students different responsibilities (e.g., vocabulary, illustrations, discussion leader, summary). For older students, the guided questions form can incorporate time period, plot, setting, descriptive language, symbols, and themes—with page references to highlight the author's

FIGURE 3.4
Book Circle Guided Reading

Question	What I can talk about in our group discussion
What was the main idea in what I read?	
What important vocabulary should I point out?	
What should I read aloud to show something that was interesting, powerful, funny, puzzling, or important from the text?	
What "pictures in my head" did this reading create?	
What other reading, movie, or picture does this remind me of?	
What should our group do next, now that we have read this?	

FIGURE 3.5
Movie Critics Activity

Grade Level	Clips/Video	Assignment for Small Groups
Elementary School	Video of illustrated book such as *Pete the Cat: I Love My White Shoes* (Dean & Litwin, 2008) shown to whole class.	Discuss how Pete felt about his shoes. Why did he always feel so happy? What is something that makes you happy? In your group, change the words to the song to something your group loves about school.
	Movie of *Akeelah and the Bee* (Fishburne & Atchison, 2006) shown to whole class.	Discuss how Akeelah felt at the beginning of the movie about what she could do. What changed for Akeelah, and why do you think she decided to compete in the spelling bee? What did her mom mean when she said that Akeelah had 50,000 teachers? What do you think about what Akeelah did for Dylan during the spelling bee?
Middle/High School	*Boycott* (Twain & Johnson, 2001) Martin Luther King Jr.'s "Been to the Mountaintop" speech (1968; available online) *A History of The Civil Rights Movement* (Schlessinger Media, 2007) *The Rosa Parks Story* (Bassett & Dash, 2003) *March On!* (King Farris & Ladd, 2008)	Each small group views a different video. In small groups, discuss which events were important in the movie you watched. Create a timeline of those events. Visually represent cause and effect events (arrest of Rosa Parks → bus boycott).
High School	*Freedom Writers* (Paramount, 2007) *Stand and Deliver* (Warner Home Video, 1988) *Dead Poets Society* (Touchstone Home Video, 1989) *Mr. Holland's Opus* (Buena Vista Home Entertainment,1995)	After viewing the movie, ask students to critique the realistic nature of the classrooms portrayed. Is it similar or different from their own experiences? How? What part should be featured on a movie trailer to snag a potential viewer's interest? Have students video interview each other as if they were emerging from the movie theater: What did you think? What was the most powerful message? Would you advise your friends to see this movie?

style—as well as information on the author's background. (See also Daniels, 2002; Candler, n.d., for background on book circles and other models for implementing book circles, including working with nonfiction texts.)

Movie Critics. This activity can be done a number of ways, depending on the age of the students (see Figure 3.5). The basic strategy is to show students a video, video clip, or full-length movie, and then have small groups of students discuss the video and rate it on several attributes, depending on the genre. The small groups report back to the larger group about their discussion. If groups watched different but related videos, the discussion might center around how the videos were alike and different.

Individual Instruction

As Opitz and Ford noted in *Engaging Minds in the Classroom*, "Individual instruction is perhaps one of the best ways to address and encourage student interest and choice which leads to joyful learning" (2014, p. 58). When we plan individual work for students, we can incorporate peer support while developing personal skills.

Connecting Self to Others

As noted throughout this book, research underlines the importance of choice and self-selection in students' independent work; both increase learner motivation and attitudes (Weih, 2008) as well as skill development (Flood, Lapp, & Fisher, 2003). As students watch others and test their own skills, they discover their strengths, interests, and personal joy in learning. The activities I recommend strengthen individual skills, allow for choice, and provide fun instruction for all students.

What's My History? Knowing about language transforms vocabulary study from memorization to engagement. Delving into word history allows individuals to tap into their curiosity about words and can be adapted for all grade levels. For this activity, assign students (or have them self-select) word histories to research and share with the class. For younger students, this may incorporate vocabulary already being taught or being used in different content areas to strengthen understanding and mastery. Students can use books (e.g., *The Merriam-Webster New Book of Word Histories*, 1991) or websites (e.g., http://www.fun-with-words.com/etymology.html or http://www.alphadictionary.com/articles) as resources. Providing students with print and online resources challenges them to uncover a good story and capitalizes on their interest in and use of technology. Follow-up activities might include creating a class dictionary (print

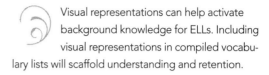

Visual representations can help activate background knowledge for ELLs. Including visual representations in compiled vocabulary lists will scaffold understanding and retention.

or online), enhanced with visual representations, or writing assignments that incorporate the studied vocabulary.

Classified Information. This activity can be completed with a local daily newspaper or by a simple Internet search (i.e., lost and found + local city), making it relatively inexpensive. It is appropriate for all grade levels. For this activity, distribute text of lost and found ads; as a writing assignment, students may

• Develop interview questions relating to lost or found items, interview another student who pretends to be the resource, and write a report about the event.

• Use the advertisement as a writing prompt to invent a background for the event.

Now that you've learned about the power of joyful learning—what it is, why it is so beneficial, how to use it in your classroom, and how it applies to language arts instruction—you may still have questions. Chapter 4 is designed to address concerns you may have about incorporating this approach within other education initiatives.

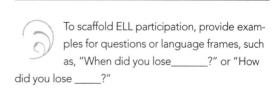

To scaffold ELL participation, provide examples for questions or language frames, such as, "When did you lose_____?" or "How did you lose _____?"

CHAPTER 4

Using Joyful Learning to Support Education Initiatives

The preceding chapters suggested ways to approach instruction that engages, motivates, and brings joy both to you and to your students. Some questions may still linger, however, and the purpose of this chapter is to address concerns you may have about incorporating this approach within other education initiatives.

I often offer workshops in how to actively engage students in becoming more efficient and accurate spellers. As teachers do word sorts, word hunts, and other hands-on activities (Fresch & Wheaton, 2002), they get excited about the potential to try something new in their classrooms. But invariably, at the end of the session, I often hear, "I love this approach, but *where do you get the words*?" Complex ideas can be mulled over and new approaches appreciated, but the nuts and bolts of the reality of teaching linger. The fundamental question remains: How do you make this happen?

How Can Joyful Learning Be Implemented Within RTI Frameworks?

The Response to Intervention (RTI) initiative focuses on early assessment and intervention. Evidence-based practices are employed to help students improve in problematic areas. Within the written, oral, and visual language arts there are many research-based strategies; the point of this book is to show you how to tweak these practices to create joyful learning. Consider the adage "if you do what you've always done, you'll get what you've always gotten" (attributed, variously, to Aristotle, Abraham Lincoln, Mark Twain, and Tony Robbins). More of the same instruction will not move students back from Tier 2 to Tier 1. Rather, we need to rethink how we are reaching and teaching struggling students. The strategies suggested in Chapter 3 require a different approach to teaching language arts. They require the teacher to be the "decision maker, not disseminator" (Howard, 2009, p. 15).

With joyful learning we can reach learners whom we may have failed to reach earlier or in other ways. You may be wondering if the strategies are too complex or demand too much of struggling learners. I argue that they do not; putting a new twist on learning and using language arts might be just what these students need. Rather than simplifying and restricting what we teach, we must open the world of real learning and wonderment to all students.

 This is a common concern when teaching ELLs. However, ELLs report more frequent use of metacognitive reading strategies than native-English-speaking students (Mokhtari & Sheorey, 2002), so there is no need to restrict what you teach!

How Does Joyful Learning Correlate to Standards?

The Common Core State Standards require instruction in English language arts across subjects, as stated

> in history/social studies, science, and technical subjects. Just as students must learn to read, write, speak, listen, and use language effectively in a variety of content areas, so too must the Standards specify the literacy skills and understandings required for college and career readiness in multiple disciplines. (National Governors Association Center for Best Practices, Council of Chief State School Officers, 2010, p. 3)

The standards describe *what* we teach, not *how* we teach. The strategies I provide in Chapter 3 fit perfectly with goals for all students (see Figure 4.1,

p. 47). Implementing these strategies not only meets the standards but also addresses your students' individual needs.

How Does Joyful Learning Address Achievement Gaps?

Joyful learning has the power to close achievement gaps in language arts. Through developing students' background knowledge in engaging ways, we can "strengthen both language competence and the ability to think in abstract ways" (Williams, 2003, p. 4). The potential to connect all students to learning, wherever they are developmentally or academically, is a beginning step in closing the gap. To move students forward, we need instructional strategies that are flexible enough to differentiate, but also rigorous. Although achievement gaps are complex and attributable to several factors, "at the end of the day, isn't all academic learning really just a means to growing healthy, socially adept, and emotionally aware individuals who can seek happiness by reaching their potential?" (Dooly, Flint, Holbrook, May, & Albers, 2012, p. 80). We can help students grow and develop as competent language arts users if we show them both the purposefulness and the fun in participating in reading, writing, listening, speaking, viewing, and representing ideas visually. Only careful planning can achieve such growth.

How Does Joyful Learning Support the Focus on Accountability and Assessment?

We need to consider how we define "test" and "assess." Remembering that *to assess* means "to sit beside" can help us keep our role as teachers in perspective. Sitting down with our students to assess progress, to celebrate success, and to change and to set goals can be a joyful process rather than a punitive one. Students need motivation and "academic perseverance" to improve (Farrington et al., 2012). Making students active participants in the assessment process

The focus on assessment extends to language acquisition. We must make students active participants and celebrate linguistic and academic development. With a deeper understanding of their language and literacy skills, we can provide purposeful instruction.

FIGURE 4.1
Meeting the Standards Through Joyful Learning Activities

Activity	Language Arts Area	Content Area Connections
Career Day	Listening, speaking	Social studies, math, science
Night at the Museum	Reading, writing, speaking, listening, viewing	Social studies, science
Learning Centers	Reading, writing, speaking, listening, viewing, visual representation	Language arts, social studies, math, science
Book Jacket Design	Reading, writing, visual representation, listening, speaking	Language arts, social studies, math, science can be connected by selecting books from a particular area of the curriculum
News at Six	Reading, writing, speaking, listening, viewing, visual representation	Language arts, social studies, math, science
Poetry Machine	Reading, writing, viewing, speaking, listening	Language arts
Book Circles	Reading, writing, listening, speaking	Language arts, other content areas depending on text selection
Movie Critics	Viewing, listening, speaking, writing	Language arts, other content areas depending on video selection
What's My History?	Viewing, listening, speaking, writing	Language arts, other content areas depending on vocabulary selection
Classified Information	Reading, writing, speaking	Social studies

has important implications related to the success of our instruction and their learning (Hopkins, 1979). Assessments should not be simply an aggregate of data that makes the individual student invisible; rather, they should illuminate the strengths and needs of our students and help guide us in creating purposeful instruction.

How Does Joyful Learning Relate to the Emphases on New Literacies and Media Use?

One sure-fire way to bring joy to learning is to capitalize on and use that with which students are both familiar and comfortable. Their growing interest and finesse with new literacies (i.e., the literacies we use to read and use various electronic forms of print and images) suggest a new way to tap into students' interests. Expecting students to use new literacies means far more than knowing how to "technologize schoolwork" (Vasquez, 2010, p. 2): it calls on us to think "of new ways of engaging as literate learners" (Vasquez, 2010, 2). Language arts provide numerous opportunities for students to do just that. They can participate in diverse media projects that incorporate all of the language arts—such as using digital storytelling apps, creating podcasts, animating information learned, attending virtual field trips, and reading and creating graphic novels. Students approach these projects with technological skills that we may not even know they possess, but that can be highlighted by innovative projects. This type of work also prepares our students for lives outside and beyond their school years (Bomer, Zoch, David, & Ok, 2010).

How do we best support our diverse student populations, including ELLs?

When discussing assessment, one population rarely served by aggregated data is our English language learners. Numbers do not show the richness of story or the ability to discuss what may be inherent in some cultures. However, using those skills in a joyful classroom can make the difference in how our ELL students engage, value, and learn the English language arts. Because language arts offer so many different ways to learn and show mastery, we can reach and teach any student. Each of the strategies in Chapter 3 can be tailored to include ELL students:

 • Night at the Museum is a good way for students to talk about their families and cultures.

- What's My History? could incorporate having students research English words that come from their mother language (e.g., Spanish with words such as *alligator, canoe, chocolate, rodeo, shack*).

- Movie Critics could allow students to watch films with subtitles in their home language so they can fully participate in the activity.

Visual representations can speak volumes where words are not yet available to a learner. With a little tweak here and there, we can include our ELL students in a rich and joyful language arts classroom.

Conclusion

My hope in writing this book is to have joyful teaching and learning become a way of life for you. Look through the lens of "Do I want to teach this?" and "Do they want to learn in this way?" If you get a *no* or even a *maybe* to either of these questions, consider rethinking how you can put the joy into that lesson. You may need to look at your students in new ways. What strengths do they show in these lessons that may not have been obvious before? How can you nudge that along? Sometimes we miss the forest for the trees and make assumptions. Can you *not* judge a book by its cover? Can you be surprised and find joy that you bring to your students? I hope so!

References

Andrade, H.L., Wang, X., Du, Y., & Akawi, R. L. (2009). Rubric-referenced self-assessment and self-efficacy for writing. *Journal of Educational Research, 103*, 287–301. http://dx.doi .org/10.3200/JOER.102.4.287-302

Bassett, A. (Producer), & Dash, J. (Director). (2003). *The Rosa Parks story* [Televison movie]. USA: Xenon Pictures.

Beaty, J. J. (2013). *50 early childhood literacy strategies* (3rd ed.). Boston: Pearson.

Beck, I. L., & McKeown, M. G. (1996). Questioning the author: A yearlong classroom implementation to engage students with text. *Elementary School Journal, 96*, 385–414. http://dx .doi.org/10.1086/461835

Behrman, E. H. (2004). Writing in the physical education class. *JOPERD, 75*(8), 22–26, 32.

Bomer, R., Zoch, M. P., David, A. D., & Ok, H. (2010). New literacies in the material world. *Language Arts, 88*(1), 9–20.

Cambourne, B. (1988). *The whole story: Natural learning and the acquisition of literacy in the classroom.* New York: Scholastic.

Candler, L. (n.d.). *Literature circle models.* Retrieved from http://www.lauracandler.com /strategies/litcirclemodels.php

Clarke, L. W., & Whitney, E. (2009). Walking in their shoes: Using multiple-perspectives texts as a bridge to critical literacy. *The Reading Teacher, 62*, 530–534. http://dx.doi.org/10.1598 /RT.62.6.7

Commonwealth of Australia. (2002a). *Codes of visual text.* Retrieved from http://www.myread .org/monitoring_codes.htm

Commonwealth of Australia. (2002b). *Critical analysis using clever cloze.* Retrieved from http:// www.myread.org/guide_cloze.htm

Culham, R. (2009). *Getting started with the traits: 3–5: Writing lessons, activities, scoring guides, and more for successfully launching trait-based instruction in your classroom.* New York: Scholastic.

Cunningham, P. M., & Allington, R. L. (1999). *Classrooms that work: They can all read and write* (2nd ed.). New York: Longman.

Daniels, H. (2002). *Literature circles: Voice and choice in book clubs and reading groups.* Portland, ME: Stenhouse.

Dean, J., & Litwin, E. (2008). *Pete the cat: I love my white shoes.* New York: HarperCollins.

Dewey, J. (1916). *Democracy and education.* New York: Macmillan.

Dockter, J., Haug, D., & Lewis, C. (2010). Redefining rigor: Critical engagement, digital media, and the new English Language Arts. *Journal of Adolescent & Adult Literacy, 53,* 418–420. http://dx.doi.org/10.1598/JAAL.53.5.7

Donoghue, M. R. (2009). *Language arts: Integrating skills for classroom teaching.* Thousand Oaks, CA: Sage.

Dooly, C. M., Flint, A. S., Holbrook, T., May, L., & Albers, P. (2012). Baby steps: Development as incremental process. *Language Arts, 90,* 79–81.

Duffelmeyer, R. (1994). Effective anticipation guide statements for learning from expository prose. *Journal of Reading, 37,* 452–457.

Farrington, C. A., Roderick, M., Allensworth, E., Nagaoka, J., Keyes, T. S., Johnson, D.W., & Beechum, N. O. (2012). *Teaching adolescents to become learners. The role of noncognitive factors in shaping school performance: A critical literature review.* Chicago: University of Chicago Consortium on Chicago School Research.

Fishburne, L. (Producer), & Atchison, D. (Director). (2006). *Akeelah and the bee* [Motion picture]. USA: Lionsgate Films.

Flood, J., Lapp, D., & Fisher, D. (2003). Reading comprehension instruction. In J. Flood, D. Lapp, J. R. Squire, & J. M. Jensen (Eds.), *Handbook of research on teaching the English language arts* (2nd ed., pp. 931–941). Mahwah, NJ: Erlbaum.

Fluckiger, J. (2010). Single point rubric: A tool for responsible student self-assessment. *Delta Kappa Gamma Bulletin, 76*(4), 18–25.

Freebody, P. (2005). Literacy teaching practice: Participation. *Australian Journal of Language and Literacy, 28*(3), 195–202.

Fresch, M. J. (2001). Journal entries as a window into spelling knowledge. *The Reading Teacher, 54,* 500–513.

Fresch, M. J., & Wheaton, A. (2002). *Teaching and assessing spelling: Striking the balance between whole-class and individualized spelling.* New York: Scholastic.

Frey, B. B., & Schmitt, V. L. (2010). Teachers' classroom assessment practices. *Middle Grades Research Journal, 5,* 107–117.

Fulghum, R. (1991). *Uh-oh: Some observations from both sides of the refrigerator door.* New York: Random House.

Genesee, F., Lindholm-Leary, K., Saunders, W., & Christian, D. (2005). English language learners in U.S. schools: An overview of research findings. *Journal of Education for Students Placed At Risk, 10*(4), 363–385.

Goodman, Y., Watson, D., & Burke, C. (1987). *Reading miscue inventory: Alternative procedures.* Katonah, NY: Owens.

Grainger, T. (2005). Teachers as writers: Learning together. *English in Education, 39*(1), 75–87. http://dx.doi.org/10.1111/j.1754-8845.2005.tb00611.x

Graves, D. (1983). *Writing: Teachers & children at work.* Portsmouth, NH: Heinemann.

Graves, M. F., & Watts-Taffe, S. (2008). For the love of words: Fostering word consciousness in young readers. *The Reading Teacher, 62,* 185–193. http://dx.doi.org/10.1598/RT.62.3.1

Grymonpré, K., Cohn, A., & Solomon, S. (2012). Getting past "just because": Teaching writing in science class. *Science Scope, 35*(5), 24–31.

Haley, A. (1976). *Roots: The saga of an American family.* New York: Doubleday.

Halliday, M. A. K. (1975). *Learning how to mean: Explorations in the development of language.* New York: Elsevier.

Hancock, M. (2007). *Language arts: Extending the possibilities.* Boston: Pearson.

Harste, J. C., & Burke, C. (1988). *Creating classrooms for authors.* Portsmouth, NH: Heinemann.

Hobbs, W. (2004, September). *Keynote*. Presentation at Rocky Mountain Children's Literature Conference, University of Northern Colorado, Greeley, CO.

Hoffman, J. V. (1992). Critical reading and thinking across the curriculum. *Language Arts, 69*, 121–124.

Hopkins, C. J. (1979). Using every-pupil response techniques in reading instruction. *The Reading Teacher, 3*, 173–175.

Howard, M. (2009). *RTI from all sides: What every teachers needs to know*. Portsmouth, NH: Heinemann.

Hoyt, L. (2007). *Interactive read alouds* (series). Portsmouth, NH: Heinemann.

Jacobowitz, T., & Sudol, K. A. (2010). Literacy strategies that promote democratic skills, attitudes, and behaviors in the social studies classroom. *Social Studies Research and Practice, 5*(3), 62–73.

Jalongo, M. R., Dragich, D., Conrad, N. K., & Zhang, A. (2002). Using wordless picture books to support emergent literacy. *Early Childhood Education Journal, 29*, 167–177. http://dx.doi.org/10.1023/A:1014584509011

King Farris, C., & Ladd, L. (2008). *March on! The day my brother Martin changed the world* [DVD]. New York: Weston Woods.

Louden, W., Rohl, M., Pugh, C. B., Brown, C., Cairney, T., Elderfield, J. . . ., & Rowe, K. (2005). *In teachers' hands: Effective literacy teaching practices in the early years of schooling*. Retrieved from http://inteachershands.education.ecu.edu.au/

Merriam-Webster. (1991). *The Merriam-Webster new book of word histories*. Springfield, MA: Author.

Methe, S. A., & Hintze, J. M. (2003). Evaluating teacher modeling as a strategy to increase student reading behavior. *School Psychology Review, 32*, 617–623.

Mokhtari, K., & Sheorey, R. (2002). Measuring ESL students' awareness of reading strategies. *Journal of Developmental Education, 25*(3), 2–10.

Morris, D., Bloodgood, J. W., Perney, J., Frye, E.M., Kucan, L., Trathen, W., Ward, D., & Schlagal, R. (2011). Validating craft knowledge: An empirical examination of elementary-grade students' performance on an informal reading assessment. *Elementary School Journal, 112*, 205–233. http://dx.doi.org/10.1086/661522

Murphy, S. (2012). Reclaiming pleasure in the teaching of reading. *Language Arts, 89*, 318–328.

Nation, I. S. P. (2005). Teaching and learning vocabulary. In E. Hinkel (Ed.), *Handbook of research in second language teaching and learning* (pp. 581–596). Mahwah, NJ: Erlbaum.

National Endowment for the Humanities. (n.d.). *All together now: Collaborations in poetry writing*. Retrieved from http://edsitement.neh.gov/lesson-plan/all-together-now-collaborations-poetry-writing#section-16759

National Governors Association Center for Best Practices, Council of Chief State School Officers. (2010). *Common core state standards*. Washington DC: Author. Retrieved from http://www.corestandards.org/the-standards

Ogle, D. M. (1986). K-W-L: A teaching model that develops active reading of expository text. *The Reading Teacher, 39*, 564–570. http://dx.doi.org/10.1598/RT.39.6.11

Ogle, D. & Beers, J. (2004). *Engaging in the language arts*. Boston: Pearson.

Opitz, M. F., & Ford, M. P. (2014). *Engaging minds in the classroom: The surprising power of joy*. Alexandria, VA: ASCD.

Opitz, M. F., Ford, M. P., & Erekson, J. A. (2011). *Accessible assessment: How 9 sensible techniques can power data-driven reading instruction*. Portsmouth, NH: Heinemann.

Opitz, M. F., & Zbaracki, M. D. (2004). *Listen hear! 25 effective listening comprehension strategies*. Portsmouth, NH: Heinemann.

Peterson, R., & Eds, M. (1991). *Grand conversations*: New York: Scholastic.

Pink, D. (2009). *Drive: The surprising truth about what motivates us*. New York: Riverhead.

Pohan, C. (2000). Practical ideas for teaching children about prejudice, discrimination, and social justice through literature and a standards-based curriculum. *Multicultural Perspectives, 2*(2), 24–28. http://dx.doi.org/10.1207/S15327892MCP0201_7

Primary sources: America's teachers on America's schools. A project of Scholastic and the Bill &
Melinda Gates Foundation. (2010). New York: Scholastic and Bill & Melinda Gates Foundation. Retrieved from http://www.governor.wa.gov/oeo/educators/scholastic_gates_report.pdf

Raphael, T. E., & Au, K. H. (2005). QAR: Enhancing comprehension and test taking across
grades and content areas. *The Reading Teacher, 59,* 206–221. http://dx.doi.org/10.1598
/RT.59.3.1

Rasinski, T. (2013). Informal vocabulary inventory. Retrieved from http://www.timrasinski.com

Reznitskaya, A., Anderson, R. C., McNurlen, B., Nguyen-Jahiel, K., Archodidou, R. C., & Kim,
S. (2001). Influence of oral discussion on written argument. *Discourse Processes, 32*(2–3),
155–175. http://dx.doi.org/10.1080/0163853X.2001.9651596

Romeo, L. (2008). Informal writing assessment linked to instruction: A continuous process for
teachers, students, and parents. *Reading & Writing Quarterly: Overcoming Learning Difficul-
ties, 24,* 25–51. http://dx.doi.org/10.1080/10573560701753070

Rowling, J. K. (1997). *Harry Potter and the philosopher's stone.* London: Bloomsbury.

Rueda, R. (2011). *The 3 dimensions of improving student performance.* New York: Teachers
College Press.

Schlagal, R. (1992). Patterns of orthographic development in intermediate grades. In S. Tem-
pleton & D. R. Bear (Eds.), *Development of orthographic knowledge and the foundations of
literacy: A memorial festschrift for Edmund H. Henderson* (pp. 31–52). Hillsdale, NJ: Erlbaum.

Schlessinger Media. (Producer). (2007). *A history of the civil rights movement* [DVD]. Available
from http://www4091.ssldomain.com/smavideo/store/index.cfm

Slavin, R. E., & Cooper, R. (1999). Improving intergroup relations: Lessons learning from cooperative learning programs. *Journal of Social Issues, 55,* 647–663. http://dx.doi.org/10.1111
/0022-4537.00140

Smith, F. (1988). *Joining the literacy club.* Portsmouth, NH: Heinemann.

Smith, F. (1994). *Understanding reading: A psycholinguistic analysis of reading and learning to
read.* Hillsdale, NJ: Erlbaum.

Stead, T. (2006). *Reality checks: Teaching reading comprehension with nonfiction K–5.* Portland,
ME: Stenhouse.

Sweeny, S. (2010).Writing for the instant messaging and text messaging generation: Using new
literacies to support writing instruction. *Language Arts, 54,* 121–130.

Tomlinson, C. (2001). *How to differentiate instruction in mixed-ability classrooms* (2nd ed.). Alexandria, VA: ASCD.

Tortello, R. (2004). Tableaux vivants in the literature classroom. *The Reading Teacher, 58,*
206–208. http://dx.doi.org/10.1598/RT.58.2.8

Twain, N. (Producer), & Johnson, C. (Director). (2001). *Boycott: Montgomery, Alabama, 1965* [Tele-
vision movie]. USA: HBO.

Vasquez, V. (2010). iPods, puppy dogs, and podcasts: Imagining literacy instruction for the 21st
century. *School Talk, 15*(2), 1–2.

Wagner, L., & Lilly, D. H. (1999). Asking the experts: Engaging students in self-assessment and
goal setting through the use of portfolios. *Assessment for Effective Instruction, 25*(1), 31–43.

Weih, T. G. (2008). A book club sheds light on boys and reading. *Middle School Journal, 40*(1), 19–25.

Whatley, A., & Canalis, J. (2002). Creating learning communities through literacy. *Language Arts,
79,* 478–487.

Wigfield, A., & Eccles, J. (2002). *Development of achievement motivation.* San Diego, CA: Academic
Press.

Williams, B. (Ed.). (2003). *Closing the achievement gap: A vision for changing beliefs and practices*
(2nd ed.). Alexandria, VA: ASCD.

Williams, T. L. (2007). "Reading" the painting: Exploring visual literacy in the primary grades.
The Reading Teacher, 60, 636–642. http://dx.doi.org/10.1598/RT.60.7.4

Index

Note: The letter *f* following a page number denotes a figure.

About the Author

Mary Jo Fresch is a professor in the Department of Teaching and Learning at Ohio State University at Marion. Her research focuses on the developmental aspect of literacy learning. Mary Jo is the author of scholarly articles and books for teachers. She may be contacted at fresch.1@osu.edu.

About the Editors

Michael F. Opitz is professor emeritus of reading education at the University of Northern Colorado, where he taught undergraduate and graduate courses. An author and literacy consultant, Michael provides inservice and staff development sessions and presents at state and international conferences and also works with elementary school teachers to plan, teach, and evaluate lessons focused on different aspects of literacy. He is the author and coauthor of numerous books, articles, and reading programs.

Michael P. Ford is the chair and a professor in the Department of Literacy and Language at the University of Wisconsin Oshkosh, where he teaches undergraduate and graduate courses. He is a former Title I reading and 1st grade teacher. Michael is the author of 5 books and more than 30 articles. Michael has worked with teachers throughout the country. His work with the international school network has included staff development presentations in the Middle East, Europe, Africa, South America, and Central America.

Friends and colleagues for more than two decades, Opitz and Ford began working together as a result of their common reading education interests. Through their publications and presentations, they continue to help educators reach readers through thoughtful, purposeful instruction grounded in practical theory.

Related ASCD Resources:
Engaging and Joyful Teaching and Learning
in English Language Arts

At the time of publication, the following ASCD resources were available (ASCD stock numbers appear in parentheses). For up-to-date information about ASCD resources, go to www.ascd.org.

ASCD EDge Group
Exchange ideas and connect with other educators interested in differentiated instruction on the social networking site ASCD EDge™ at http://ascdedge.ascd.org/

Print Products
Building Student Literacy Through Sustained Silent Reading by Steve Gardiner (#105027)

Creating Literacy-Rich Schools for Adolescents by Gay Ivey and Douglas Fisher (#105142)

Differentiated Literacy Coaching: Scaffolding for Student and Teacher Success by Mary Catherine Moran (#107053)

Effective Literacy Coaching: Building Expertise and a Culture of Literacy by Shari Frost, Roberta Buhle, and Camille Blachowicz (#109044)

Engaging the Whole Child: Reflections on Best Practices in Learning, Teaching, and Leadership edited by Marge Scherer and the Educational Leadership Staff (#109103)

Essential Ingredients: Recipes for Teaching Writing by Sandra Worsham (#101241)

Flip Your Classroom: Reach Every Student in Every Class Every Day Jonathan Bergmann and Aaron Sams (#112060)

Learning and Leading with Habits of Mind: 16 Essential Characteristics for Success edited by Arthur L. Costa and Bena Kallick (#108008)

Literacy Leadership for Grades 5–12 by Rosemarye Taylor and Valerie Doyle Collins (#103022)

Literacy Strategies for Grades 4–12: Reinforcing the Threads of Reading by Karen Tankersley (#104428)

The Multiple Intelligences of Reading and Writing: Making the Words Come Alive by Thomas Armstrong (#102280)

Research-Based Methods of Reading Instruction for English Language Learners, Grades K–4 by Sylvia Linan-Thompson and Sharon Vaughn (#108002)

Research-Based Methods of Reading Instruction, Grades K–3 by Sharon Vaughn and Sylvia Linan-Thompson (#104134)

Teaching Beginning Reading and Writing with the Picture Word Inductive Model by Emily F. Calhoun (#199025)

The Threads of Reading: Strategies for Literacy Development (2003) by Karen Tankersley (#103316)

 The Whole Child Initiative helps schools and communities create learning environments that allow students to be healthy, safe, engaged, supported, and challenged. To learn more about other books and resources that relate to the whole child, visit www.wholechildeducation.org.

For more information: send e-mail to member@ascd.org; call 1-800-933-2723 or 703-578-9600, press 2; send a fax to 703-575-5400; or write to Information Services, ASCD, 1703 N. Beauregard St., Alexandria, VA 22311-1714 USA.